100 Best *Business Books*
Reading Log

Name: _____

Email: _____

Cell Phone: _____

This book is copyright protected. Please do not reproduce in either electronic means or in printed format except for your explicit personal use. This means that copying this book is prohibited and not allowed without permission from the author.
All Rights Reserved

Title	Author
○ How to Win Friends and Influence People	*Dale Carnegie*
○ The 7 Habits of Highly Effective People: Powerful Lessons in Personal Change	*Stephen R. Covey*
○ Think and Grow Rich	*Napoleon Hill*
○ Good to Great: Why Some Companies Make the Leap... and Others Don't	*James C. Collins*
○ Getting Things Done: The Art of Stress-Free Productivity	*David Allen*
○ Rich Dad, Poor Dad	*Robert T. Kiyosaki*
○ The 4-Hour Workweek	*Timothy Ferriss*
○ Influence: The Psychology of Persuasion	*Robert B. Cialdini*
○ Freakonomics: A Rogue Economist Explores the Hidden Side of Everything	*Steven D. Levitt*
○ The 48 Laws of Power	*Robert Greene*
○ Thinking, Fast and Slow	*Daniel Kahneman*
○ The Goal: A Process of Ongoing Improvement	*Eliyahu M. Goldratt*
○ The E-Myth Revisited: Why Most Small Businesses Don't Work and What to Do About It	*Michael E. Gerber*
○ Emotional Intelligence 2.0	*Travis Bradberry*
○ Rework	*Jason Fried*
○ The Lean Startup: How Today's Entrepreneurs Use Continuous Innovation to Create Radically Successful Businesses	*Eric Ries*
○ Predictably Irrational: The Hidden Forces That Shape Our Decisions	*Dan Ariely*
○ The Richest Man in Babylon	*George S. Clason*
○ Made to Stick: Why Some Ideas Survive and Others Die	*Chip Heath*
○ The Tipping Point: How Little Things Can Make a Big Difference	*Malcolm Gladwell*

	Title	Author
○	Steve Jobs	*Walter Isaacson*
○	Purple Cow: Transform Your Business by Being Remarkable	*Seth Godin*
○	Drive: The Surprising Truth About What Motivates Us	*Daniel H. Pink*
○	Strengths Finder 2.0	*Tom Rath*
○	First, Break All the Rules: What the World's Greatest Managers Do Differently	*Marcus Buckingham*
○	The Speed of Trust: The One Thing that Changes Everything	*Stephen M.R. Covey*
○	Delivering Happiness: A Path to Profits, Passion, and Purpose	*Tony Hsieh*
○	Liar's Poker	*Michael Lewis*
○	Tribes We Need You to Lead Us. Seth Godin	*Seth Godin*
○	The Art of War	*Sun Tzu*
○	The Big Short: Inside the Doomsday Machine	*Michael Lewis*
○	Getting to Yes: Negotiating Agreement Without Giving In	*Roger Fisher*
○	The Black Swan: The Impact of the Highly Improbable	*Nassim Nicholas Taleb*
○	The Art of the Start: The Time-Tested, Battle-Hardened Guide for Anyone Starting Anything	*Guy Kawasaki*
○	Blue Ocean Strategy: How to Create Uncontested Market Space and Make the Competition Irrelevant	*W. Chan Kim*
○	The Dip: A Little Book That Teaches You When to Quit	*Seth Godin*
○	The Innovator's Dilemma: The Revolutionary Book that Will Change the Way You Do Business	*Clayton M. Christensen*
○	Built to Last: Successful Habits of Visionary Companies	*James C. Collins*
○	Linchpin: Are You Indispensable?	*Seth Godin*
○	Crucial Conversations: Tools for Talking When Stakes Are High	*Kerry Patterson*
○	Quiet: The Power of Introverts in a World That Can't Stop Talking	*Susan Cain*
○	The Five Dysfunctions of a Team: A Leadership Fable	*Patrick Lencioni*
○	In Search of Excellence	*Thomas J. Peters*
○	The Intelligent Investor	*Benjamin Graham*

○	Never Eat Alone: And Other Secrets to Success, One Relationship at a Time	Keith Ferrazzi
○	Marketing Management	Philip Kotler
○	SuperFreakonomics: Global Cooling, Patriotic Prostitutes And Why Suicide Bombers Should Buy Life Insurance	Steven D. Levitt
○	When Genius Failed: The Rise and Fall of Long-Term Capital Management	Roger Lowenstein
○	The 21 Irrefutable Laws of Leadership: Follow Them and People Will Follow You	John C. Maxwell
○	Against the Gods: The Remarkable Story of Risk	Peter L. Bernstein
○	Explosive Growth: A Few Things I Learned While Growing To 100 Million Users - And Losing $78 Million	Cliff Lerner
○	All Marketers Are Liars	Seth Godin
○	Crossing the Chasm: Marketing and Selling High-Tech Products to Mainstream Customers	Geoffrey A. Moore
○	Moneyball: The Art of Winning an Unfair Game	Michael Lewis
○	Organisational Anatomy	Oleg Konovalov
○	The Millionaire Mind	Thomas J. Stanley
○	Business Model Generation	Alexander Osterwalder
○	Founders at Work: Stories of Startups' Early Days	Jessica Livingston
○	Positioning: The Battle for Your Mind: How to Be Seen and Heard in the Overcrowded Marketplace	Al Ries
○	Winning Intl	Jack Welch
○	You Couldn't Have Told Me Before I Started My Business?	Jeff Roziere
○	The One Minute Manager	Kenneth H. Blanchard
○	Massive Action Equal Massive Results: Learn the Critical Mental Framework to Focus Your Energy, Reach Your Goals Quicker and Live an Insanely Awesome Life	Sunil Saxena
○	The Autobiography of Benjamin Franklin	Benjamin Franklin

○	Zig Ziglar's Secrets of Closing the Sale	Zig Ziglar
○	Start with Why: How Great Leaders Inspire Everyone to Take Action	Simon Sinek
○	The Greatest Salesman in the World	Og Mandino
○	Outliers: The Story of Success	Malcolm Gladwell
○	Competitive Advantage: Creating and Sustaining Superior Performance	Michael E. Porter
○	Secret to Startup Failure: Fail Fast. Fail Cheap. Fail Happy.	Sonia Lin
○	The World Is Flat: A Brief History of the Twenty-first Century	Thomas L. Friedman
○	Free: The Future of a Radical Price	Chris Anderson
○	The Long Tail: Why the Future of Business is Selling Less of More	Chris Anderson
○	Too Big to Fail: The Inside Story of How Wall Street and Washington Fought to Save the Financial System from Crisis — and Themselves	Andrew Ross Sorkin
○	What to Say When You Talk to Your Self	Shad Helmstetter
○	The Extremely Successful Salesman's Club	Chris Murray
○	The Secrets of Consulting: A Guide to Giving and Getting Advice Successfully	Gerald M. Weinberg
○	Peopleware: Productive Projects and Teams	Tom DeMarco
○	The Effective Executive: The Definitive Guide to Getting the Right Things Done	Peter F. Drucker
○	Shoe Dog: A Memoir by the Creator of NIKE	Phil Knight
○	Great by Choice: Uncertainty, Chaos, and Luck—Why Some Thrive Despite Them All	James C. Collins
○	The Undercover Economist	Tim Harford
○	Confessions of a Public Speaker	Scott Berkun
○	Never Work Again: Work Less, Earn More and Live Your Freedom	Erlend Bakke
○	Eat That Frog!: 21 Great Ways to Stop Procrastinating and Get More Done in Less Time	Brian Tracy
○	Principles of Marketing	Philip Kotler

	Title	Author
○	The Contrarian's Guide to Leadership	Steven B. Sample
○	The Ten-Day MBA : A Step-By-Step Guide To Mastering The Skills Taught In America's Top Business Schools	Steven Silbiger
○	Orbiting the Giant Hairball: A Corporate Fool's Guide to Surviving with Grace	Gordon MacKenzie
○	Social Media for the Executive	Brian E. Boyd Sr.
○	The Power of Full Engagement: Managing Energy, Not Time, Is the Key to High Performance and Personal Renewal	Jim Loehr
○	EntreLeadership: 20 Years of Practical Business Wisdom from the Trenches	Dave Ramsey
○	Launching a Leadership Revolution: Mastering the Five Levels of Influence	Chris Brady
○	Difficult Conversations: How to Discuss What Matters Most	Douglas Stone
○	Capitalism and Freedom	Milton Friedman
○	From the Ground Up: A Journey to Reimagine the Promise of America	Howard Schultz
○	It Is What It Is, Or Is It....: All About Business	Cathy Snelgrove Jeff Roziere
○	The Idea-Driven Organization: Unlocking the Power in Bottom-Up Ideas	Alan G. Robinson
○	Match in the Root Cellar: How You Can Spark a Peak Performance Culture	Chris McGoff
○	Dare to Lead	Brené Brown

Title: How to Win Friends and Influence People	

Author: Dale Carnegie

Paperback   Hardback   Audio   E-Book

| Dates:
 Started -
 Finished - | Source:
❑ Bought:
❑ Loaned From: |

Why I read this book:

This book has inspired me to read/learn/visit:

Notes:

Great Quotes:

Recommend this book to:

Title: The 7 Habits of Highly Effective People: Powerful Lessons in Personal Change

Author: Stephen R. Covey

Paperback	Hardback	Audio	E-Book

Dates:
  Started -
  Finished -
	Source:
	❑ Bought:
	❑ Loaned From:

Why I read this book:

This book has inspired me to read/learn/visit:

Notes:

Great Quotes:

Recommend this book to:

Title: Think and Grow Rich

Author: Napoleon Hill

Paperback   Hardback   Audio   E-Book

Dates:
  Started -
  Finished -
	Source:
	❑ Bought:
	❑ Loaned From:

Why I read this book:

This book has inspired me to read/learn/visit:

Notes:

Great Quotes:

Recommend this book to:

Title: Good to Great: Why Some Companies Make the Leap... and Others Don't

Author: James C. Collins

Paperback   Hardback   Audio   E-Book

Dates:
 Started -
 Finished -

Source:
❏ Bought:
❏ Loaned From:

Why I read this book:

This book has inspired me to read/learn/visit:

Notes:

Great Quotes:

Recommend this book to:

Title: Getting Things Done: The Art of Stress-Free Productivity

Author: David Allen

Paperback   Hardback   Audio   E-Book

Dates:
  Started -
  Finished -

Source:
❑ Bought:
❑ Loaned From:

Why I read this book:

This book has inspired me to read/learn/visit:

Notes:

Great Quotes:

Recommend this book to:

Title: Rich Dad, Poor Dad	
Author: Robert T. Kiyosaki	

Paperback   Hardback   Audio   E-Book

Dates:
  Started -
  Finished -
	Source:
	❏ Bought:
	❏ Loaned From:

Why I read this book:

This book has inspired me to read/learn/visit:

Notes:

Great Quotes:

Recommend this book to:

Title: The 4-Hour Workweek	
Author: Timothy Ferriss	
Paperback Hardback Audio E-Book	

Dates:
  Started -
  Finished -
	Source:
	❏ Bought:
	❏ Loaned From:

Why I read this book:	
This book has inspired me to read/learn/visit:	
Notes:	
Great Quotes:	
Recommend this book to:	

Title: Influence: The Psychology of Persuasion

Author: Robert B. Cialdini

Paperback   Hardback   Audio   E-Book

Dates:
  Started -
  Finished -
	Source:
	❏ Bought:
	❏ Loaned From:

Why I read this book:

This book has inspired me to read/learn/visit:

Notes:

Great Quotes:

Recommend this book to:

Title: Freakonomics: A Rogue Economist Explores the Hidden Side of Everything

Author: Steven D. Levitt

Paperback   Hardback   Audio   E-Book

Dates:
  Started -
  Finished -

Source:
  ☐ Bought:
  ☐ Loaned From:

Why I read this book:

This book has inspired me to read/learn/visit:

Notes:

Great Quotes:

Recommend this book to:

Title: The 48 Laws of Power

Author: Robert Greene

Paperback   Hardback   Audio   E-Book

Dates:
  Started -
  Finished -

Source:
❑ Bought:
❑ Loaned From:

Why I read this book:

This book has inspired me to read/learn/visit:

Notes:

Great Quotes:

Recommend this book to:

Title: Thinking, Fast and Slow

Author: Daniel Kahneman

Paperback   Hardback   Audio   E-Book

Dates:
  Started -
  Finished -
	Source:
	❏ Bought:
	❏ Loaned From:

Why I read this book:

This book has inspired me to read/learn/visit:

Notes:

Great Quotes:

Recommend this book to:

Title: The Goal: A Process of Ongoing Improvement	

Author: Eliyahu M. Goldratt

Paperback	Hardback	Audio	E-Book

Dates:
  Started -
  Finished -
	Source:
	❑ Bought:
	❑ Loaned From:

Why I read this book:

This book has inspired me to read/learn/visit:

Notes:

Great Quotes:

Recommend this book to:

Title: The E-Myth Revisited: Why Most Small Businesses Don't Work and What to Do About It

Author: Michael E. Gerber

Paperback   Hardback   Audio   E-Book

Dates:
 Started -
 Finished -

Source:
 ❏   Bought:
 ❏   Loaned From:

Why I read this book:

This book has inspired me to read/learn/visit:

Notes:

Great Quotes:

Recommend this book to:

Title: Emotional Intelligence 2.0	

Author: Travis Bradberry

Paperback   Hardback   Audio   E-Book

Dates:
  Started -
  Finished -
	Source:
	☐ Bought:
	☐ Loaned From:

Why I read this book:

This book has inspired me to read/learn/visit:

Notes:

Great Quotes:

Recommend this book to:

Title: Rework

Author: Jason Fried

Paperback   Hardback   Audio   E-Book

Dates:
  Started -
  Finished -
	Source:
	❏ Bought:
	❏ Loaned From:

Why I read this book:

This book has inspired me to read/learn/visit:

Notes:

Great Quotes:

Recommend this book to:

Title: The Lean Startup: How Today's Entrepreneurs Use Continuous Innovation to Create Radically Successful Businesses

Author: Eric Ries

Paperback   Hardback   Audio   E-Book

Dates:	Source:
Started -	☐ Bought:
Finished -	☐ Loaned From:

Why I read this book:

This book has inspired me to read/learn/visit:

Notes:

Great Quotes:

Recommend this book to:

Title: Predictably Irrational: The Hidden Forces That Shape Our Decisions

Author: Dan Ariely

Paperback   Hardback   Audio   E-Book

Dates:
 Started -
 Finished -

Source:
 ❏   Bought:
 ❏   Loaned From:

Why I read this book:

This book has inspired me to read/learn/visit:

Notes:

Great Quotes:

Recommend this book to:

Title: The Richest Man in Babylon	

Author: George S. Clason

Paperback   Hardback   Audio   E-Book

Dates:
  Started -
  Finished -
	Source:
	  ❏ Bought:
	  ❏ Loaned From:

Why I read this book:

This book has inspired me to read/learn/visit:

Notes:

Great Quotes:

Recommend this book to:

Title: Made to Stick: Why Some Ideas Survive and Others Die	

Author: Chip Heath

Paperback   Hardback   Audio   E-Book

Dates:
  Started -
  Finished -
	Source:
	❏ Bought:
	❏ Loaned From:

Why I read this book:

This book has inspired me to read/learn/visit:

Notes:

Great Quotes:

Recommend this book to:

Title: The Tipping Point: How Little Things Can Make a Big Difference

Author: Malcolm Gladwell

Paperback   Hardback   Audio   E-Book

Dates:	Source:
Started -	☐ Bought:
Finished -	☐ Loaned From:

Why I read this book:

This book has inspired me to read/learn/visit:

Notes:

Great Quotes:

Recommend this book to:

Title: Steve Jobs

Author: Walter Isaacson

| Paperback | Hardback | Audio | E-Book |

| Dates:
  Started -
  Finished
  - | Source:
  ☐ Bought:
  ☐ Loaned From: |

Why I read this book:

This book has inspired me to read/learn/visit:

Notes:

Great Quotes:

Recommend this book to:

Title: Purple Cow: Transform Your Business by Being Remarkable

Author: Seth Godin

Paperback   Hardback   Audio   E-Book

Dates:
  Started -
  Finished -
	Source:
	❑ Bought:
	❑ Loaned From:

Why I read this book:

This book has inspired me to read/learn/visit:

Notes:

Great Quotes:

Recommend this book to:

Title: Drive: The Surprising Truth About What Motivates Us	

Author: Daniel H. Pink

Paperback	Hardback	Audio	E-Book

Dates:
  Started -
  Finished
  -
	Source:
	❑ Bought:
	❑ Loaned From:

Why I read this book:

This book has inspired me to read/learn/visit:

Notes:

Great Quotes:

Recommend this book to:

Title: Strengths Finder 2.0

Author: Tom Rath

Paperback　　Hardback　　Audio　　E-Book

Dates: 　Started - 　Finished -	Source: 　❏　Bought: 　❏　Loaned From:

Why I read this book:

This book has inspired me to read/learn/visit:

Notes:

Great Quotes:

Recommend this book to:

Title: First, Break All the Rules: What the World's Greatest Managers Do Differently

Author: Marcus Buckingham

Paperback   Hardback   Audio   E-Book

Dates: Started - Finished -	Source: ☐ Bought: ☐ Loaned From:

Why I read this book:

This book has inspired me to read/learn/visit:

Notes:

Great Quotes:

Recommend this book to:

Title: The Speed of Trust: The One Thing that Changes Everything	

Author: Stephen M.R. Covey

Paperback   Hardback   Audio   E-Book

Dates:	Source:
Started -	☐ Bought:
Finished	☐ Loaned From:
-	

Why I read this book:

This book has inspired me to read/learn/visit:

Notes:

Great Quotes:

Recommend this book to:

| Title: Delivering Happiness: A Path to Profits, Passion, and Purpose |

| Author: Tony Hsieh |

Paperback   Hardback   Audio   E-Book

Dates:	Source:
Started -	❑ Bought:
Finished -	❑ Loaned From:

Why I read this book:

This book has inspired me to read/learn/visit:

Notes:

Great Quotes:

Recommend this book to:

Title: Liar's Poker	

Author: Michael Lewis

Paperback   Hardback   Audio   E-Book

Dates:
  Started -
  Finished
  -
	Source:
	  ❏ Bought:
	  ❏ Loaned From:

Why I read this book:

This book has inspired me to read/learn/visit:

Notes:

Great Quotes:

Recommend this book to:

Title: Tribes We Need You to Lead Us. Seth Godin	
Author: Seth Godin	
Paperback Hardback Audio E-Book	
Dates: Started - Finished -	Source: ❏ Bought: ❏ Loaned From:
Why I read this book:	
This book has inspired me to read/learn/visit:	
Notes:	
Great Quotes:	
Recommend this book to:	

Title: The Art of War

Author: Sun Tzu

Paperback   Hardback   Audio   E-Book

Dates:	Source:
Started -	☐ Bought:
Finished -	☐ Loaned From:

Why I read this book:

This book has inspired me to read/learn/visit:

Notes:

Great Quotes:

Recommend this book to:

Title: The Big Short: Inside the Doomsday Machine

Author: Michael Lewis

Paperback   Hardback   Audio   E-Book

Dates:
  Started -
  Finished -

Source:
❑ Bought:
❑ Loaned From:

Why I read this book:

This book has inspired me to read/learn/visit:

Notes:

Great Quotes:

Recommend this book to:

Title: Getting to Yes: Negotiating Agreement Without Giving In	

Author: Roger Fisher

Paperback   Hardback   Audio   E-Book

Dates: 　Started - 　Finished 　-	Source: 　❑　Bought: 　❑　Loaned From:

Why I read this book:

This book has inspired me to read/learn/visit:

Notes:

Great Quotes:

Recommend this book to:

Title: The Black Swan: The Impact of the Highly Improbable

Author: Nassim Nicholas Taleb

Paperback　　Hardback　　Audio　　E-Book

Dates:
  Started -
  Finished -

Source:
  ❑ Bought:
  ❑ Loaned From:

Why I read this book:

This book has inspired me to read/learn/visit:

Notes:

Great Quotes:

Recommend this book to:

Title: The Art of the Start: The Time-Tested, Battle-Hardened Guide for Anyone Starting Anything

Author: Guy Kawasaki

Paperback   Hardback   Audio   E-Book

Dates:	Source:
Started -	❑ Bought:
Finished -	❑ Loaned From:

Why I read this book:

This book has inspired me to read/learn/visit:

Notes:

Great Quotes:

Recommend this book to:

Title: Blue Ocean Strategy: How to Create Uncontested Market Space and Make the Competition Irrelevant				
Author: W. Chan Kim				
Paperback	Hardback		Audio	E-Book
Dates: 　Started - 　Finished -			Source: ❏　　Bought: ❏　　Loaned From:	
Why I read this book:				
This book has inspired me to read/learn/visit:				
Notes:				
Great Quotes:				
Recommend this book to:				

Title: The Dip: A Little Book That Teaches You When to Quit
Author: Seth Godin

Paperback   Hardback   Audio   E-Book

Dates:
  Started -
  Finished
  -
	Source:
	  ❏ Bought:
	  ❏ Loaned From:

Why I read this book:

This book has inspired me to read/learn/visit:

Notes:

Great Quotes:

Recommend this book to:

Title: The Innovator's Dilemma: The Revolutionary Book that Will Change the Way You Do Business	

Author: Clayton M. Christemsen

Paperback   Hardback   Audio   E-Book

Dates:
  Started -
  Finished -
	Source:
	❏ Bought:
	❏ Loaned From:

Why I read this book:

This book has inspired me to read/learn/visit:

Notes:

Great Quotes:

Recommend this book to:

Title: Built to Last: Successful Habits of Visionary Companies

Author: James C. Collins

Paperback   Hardback   Audio   E-Book

Dates:
 Started -
 Finished -

Source:
 ❏   Bought:
 ❏   Loaned From:

Why I read this book:

This book has inspired me to read/learn/visit:

Notes:

Great Quotes:

Recommend this book to:

Title: Linchpin: Are You Indispensable?	

Author: Seth Godin

Paperback   Hardback   Audio   E-Book

Dates:
  Started -
  Finished -
	Source:
	❏ Bought:
	❏ Loaned From:

Why I read this book:

This book has inspired me to read/learn/visit:

Notes:

Great Quotes:

Recommend this book to:

Title: Crucial Conversations: Tools for Talking When Stakes Are High

Author: Kerry Patterson

Paperback   Hardback   Audio   E-Book

Dates:	Source:
Started -	❏ Bought:
Finished -	❏ Loaned From:

Why I read this book:

This book has inspired me to read/learn/visit:

Notes:

Great Quotes:

Recommend this book to:

Title: Quiet: The Power of Introverts in a World That Can't Stop Talking	

Author: Susan Cain

Paperback   Hardback   Audio   E-Book

Dates:
  Started -
  Finished -
	Source:
	  ❑ Bought:
	  ❑ Loaned From:

Why I read this book:

This book has inspired me to read/learn/visit:

Notes:

Great Quotes:

Recommend this book to:

Title: The Five Dysfunctions of a Team: A Leadership Fable

Author: Patrick Lencioni

Paperback   Hardback   Audio   E-Book

Dates:
 Started -
 Finished -

Source:
 ❑   Bought:
 ❑   Loaned From:

Why I read this book:

This book has inspired me to read/learn/visit:

Notes:

Great Quotes:

Recommend this book to:

Title: In Search of Excellence	

Author: Thomas J. Peters

Paperback   Hardback   Audio   E-Book

Dates:
  Started -
  Finished -
	Source:
	❑ Bought:
	❑ Loaned From:

Why I read this book:

This book has inspired me to read/learn/visit:

Notes:

Great Quotes:

Recommend this book to:

Title: The Intelligent Investor

Author: Benjamin Graham

Paperback   Hardback   Audio   E-Book

Dates:
  Started -
  Finished -

Source:
  ❑ Bought:
  ❑ Loaned From:

Why I read this book:

This book has inspired me to read/learn/visit:

Notes:

Great Quotes:

Recommend this book to:

Title: Never Eat Alone: And Other Secrets to Success, One Relationship at a Time

Author: Keith Ferrazzi

Paperback   Hardback   Audio   E-Book

Dates:
  Started -
  Finished -

Source:
❏ Bought:
❏ Loaned From:

Why I read this book:

This book has inspired me to read/learn/visit:

Notes:

Great Quotes:

Recommend this book to:

Title: Marketing Management

Author: Philip Kotler

Paperback   Hardback   Audio   E-Book

Dates:
  Started -
  Finished -

Source:
❑ Bought:
❑ Loaned From:

Why I read this book:

This book has inspired me to read/learn/visit:

Notes:

Great Quotes:

Recommend this book to:

Title: SuperFreakonomics: Global Cooling, Patriotic Prostitutes And Why Suicide Bombers Should Buy Life Insurance	
Author: Steven D. Levitt	
Paperback Hardback Audio E-Book	

Dates:
  Started -
  Finished -
	Source:
	❑ Bought:
	❑ Loaned From:

Why I read this book:	
This book has inspired me to read/learn/visit:	
Notes:	
Great Quotes:	
Recommend this book to:	

Title: When Genius Failed: The Rise and Fall of Long-Term Capital Management

Author: Roger Lowenstein

Paperback   Hardback   Audio   E-Book

Dates:
  Started -
  Finished -

Source:
  ❏ Bought:
  ❏ Loaned From:

Why I read this book:

This book has inspired me to read/learn/visit:

Notes:

Great Quotes:

Recommend this book to:

Title: The 21 Irrefutable Laws of Leadership: Follow Them and People Will Follow You

Author: John C. Maxwell

| Paperback | Hardback | Audio | E-Book |

Dates:
  Started -
  Finished -

Source:
- ❏ Bought:
- ❏ Loaned From:

Why I read this book:

This book has inspired me to read/learn/visit:

Notes:

Great Quotes:

Recommend this book to:

Title: Against the Gods: The Remarkable Story of Risk	

Author: Peter L. Bernstein

Paperback   Hardback   Audio   E-Book

Dates:
  Started -
  Finished -
	Source:
	  ❑ Bought:
	  ❑ Loaned From:

Why I read this book:

This book has inspired me to read/learn/visit:

Notes:

Great Quotes:

Recommend this book to:

Title: Explosive Growth: A Few Things I Learned While Growing To 100 Million Users - And Losing $78 Million	

Author: Cliff Lerner

Paperback   Hardback   Audio   E-Book

Dates:
  Started -
  Finished -
	Source:
	❏ Bought:
	❏ Loaned From:

Why I read this book:

This book has inspired me to read/learn/visit:

Notes:

Great Quotes:

Recommend this book to:

Title: All Marketers Are Liars

Author: Seth Godin

Paperback	Hardback	Audio	E-Book

Dates:
  Started -
  Finished -
	Source:
	❏ Bought:
	❏ Loaned From:

Why I read this book:

This book has inspired me to read/learn/visit:

Notes:

Great Quotes:

Recommend this book to:

Title: Crossing the Chasm: Marketing and Selling High-Tech Products to Mainstream Customers

Author: Geoffrey A. Moore

Paperback   Hardback   Audio   E-Book

Dates:
  Started -
  Finished -

Source:
  ❑ Bought:
  ❑ Loaned From:

Why I read this book:

This book has inspired me to read/learn/visit:

Notes:

Great Quotes:

Recommend this book to:

Title: Moneyball: The Art of Winning an Unfair Game	

Author: Michael Lewis

Paperback   Hardback   Audio   E-Book

Dates:
  Started -
  Finished -
	Source:
	  ❏ Bought:
	  ❏ Loaned From:

Why I read this book:

This book has inspired me to read/learn/visit:

Notes:

Great Quotes:

Recommend this book to:

Title: Organisational Anatomy

Author: Oleg Konovalov

Paperback	Hardback	Audio	E-Book

Dates: 　Started - 　Finished -	Source: ❏　Bought: ❏　Loaned From:

Why I read this book:

This book has inspired me to read/learn/visit:

Notes:

Great Quotes:

Recommend this book to:

Title: The Millionaire Mind

Author: Thomas J. Stanley

Paperback   Hardback   Audio   E-Book

Dates:
  Started -
  Finished -

Source:
  ❏ Bought:
  ❏ Loaned From:

Why I read this book:

This book has inspired me to read/learn/visit:

Notes:

Great Quotes:

Recommend this book to:

Title: Business Model Generation	

Author: Alexander Osterwalder

Paperback   Hardback   Audio   E-Book

Dates:
  Started -
  Finished -

Source:
❑ Bought:
❑ Loaned From:

Why I read this book:

This book has inspired me to read/learn/visit:

Notes:

Great Quotes:

Recommend this book to:

Title: Founders at Work: Stories of Startups' Early Days

Author: Jessica Livingston

Paperback   Hardback   Audio   E-Book

Dates:
 Started -
 Finished -

Source:
☐ Bought:
☐ Loaned From:

Why I read this book:

This book has inspired me to read/learn/visit:

Notes:

Great Quotes:

Recommend this book to:

Title: Positioning: The Battle for Your Mind: How to Be Seen and Heard in the Overcrowded Marketplace
Author: Al Ries

Paperback   Hardback   Audio   E-Book

Dates: 　Started - 　Finished -	Source: ❏　Bought: ❏　Loaned From:

Why I read this book:

This book has inspired me to read/learn/visit:

Notes:

Great Quotes:

Recommend this book to:

Title: Winning Intl

Author: Jack Welch

Paperback   Hardback   Audio   E-Book

Dates:
 Started -
 Finished -

Source:
 ❑ Bought:
 ❑ Loaned From:

Why I read this book:

This book has inspired me to read/learn/visit:

Notes:

Great Quotes:

Recommend this book to:

Title: You Couldn't Have Told Me Before I Started My Business?

Author: Jeff Roziere

Paperback   Hardback   Audio   E-Book

Dates:
  Started -
  Finished -

Source:
☐ Bought:
☐ Loaned From:

Why I read this book:

This book has inspired me to read/learn/visit:

Notes:

Great Quotes:

Recommend this book to:

Title: The One Minute Manager	

Author: Kenneth H. Blanchard

Paperback   Hardback   Audio   E-Book

Dates:	Source:
Started -	❏ Bought:
Finished -	❏ Loaned From:

Why I read this book:

This book has inspired me to read/learn/visit:

Notes:

Great Quotes:

Recommend this book to:

Title: Massive Action Equal Massive Results: Learn the Critical Mental Framework to Focus Your Energy, Reach Your Goals Quicker and Live an Insanely Awesome Life

Author: Sunil Saxena

Paperback   Hardback   Audio   E-Book

Dates:
  Started -
  Finished -

Source:
❑   Bought:
❑   Loaned From:

Why I read this book:

This book has inspired me to read/learn/visit:

Notes:

Great Quotes:

Recommend this book to:

Title: The Autobiography of Benjamin Franklin

Author: Benjamin Franklin

Paperback   Hardback   Audio   E-Book

Dates:
  Started -
  Finished -

Source:
  ❏ Bought:
  ❏ Loaned From:

Why I read this book:

This book has inspired me to read/learn/visit:

Notes:

Great Quotes:

Recommend this book to:

Title: Zig Ziglar's Secrets of Closing the Sale

Author: Zig Ziglar

Paperback   Hardback   Audio   E-Book

Dates:
 Started -
 Finished -

Source:
 ❑ Bought:
 ❑ Loaned From:

Why I read this book:

This book has inspired me to read/learn/visit:

Notes:

Great Quotes:

Recommend this book to:

Title: Start with Why: How Great Leaders Inspire Everyone to Take Action	

Author: Simon Sinek

Paperback   Hardback   Audio   E-Book

Dates:
  Started -
  Finished -
	Source:
	  ❏ Bought:
	  ❏ Loaned From:

Why I read this book:

This book has inspired me to read/learn/visit:

Notes:

Great Quotes:

Recommend this book to:

Title: The Greatest Salesman in the World	
Author: Og Mandino	

Paperback	Hardback	Audio	E-Book

Dates:
  Started -
  Finished -
	Source:
	❑ Bought:
	❑ Loaned From:

Why I read this book:

This book has inspired me to read/learn/visit:

Notes:

Great Quotes:

Recommend this book to:

Title: Outliers: The Story of Success

Author: Malcolm Gladwell

Paperback   Hardback   Audio   E-Book

Dates: Started - Finished -	Source: ❏ Bought: ❏ Loaned From:

Why I read this book:

This book has inspired me to read/learn/visit:

Notes:

Great Quotes:

Recommend this book to:

Title: Competitive Advantage: Creating and Sustaining Superior Performance

Author: Michael E. Porter

Paperback   Hardback   Audio   E-Book

Dates:
  Started -
  Finished -

Source:
  ❑ Bought:
  ❑ Loaned From:

Why I read this book:

This book has inspired me to read/learn/visit:

Notes:

Great Quotes:

Recommend this book to:

Title: Secret to Startup Failure: Fail Fast. Fail Cheap. Fail Happy.

Author: Sonia Lin

Paperback   Hardback   Audio   E-Book

Dates:
  Started -
  Finished -

Source:
  ☐ Bought:
  ☐ Loaned From:

Why I read this book:

This book has inspired me to read/learn/visit:

Notes:

Great Quotes:

Recommend this book to:

Title: The World Is Flat: A Brief History of the Twenty-first Century	

Author: Thomas L. Friedman

Paperback   Hardback   Audio   E-Book

Dates:	Source:
Started -	❏ Bought:
Finished -	❏ Loaned From:

Why I read this book:

This book has inspired me to read/learn/visit:

Notes:

Great Quotes:

Recommend this book to:

Title: Free: The Future of a Radical Price

Author: Chris Anderson

Paperback   Hardback   Audio   E-Book

Dates:
  Started -
  Finished -
	Source:
	  ❑ Bought:
	  ❑ Loaned From:

Why I read this book:

This book has inspired me to read/learn/visit:

Notes:

Great Quotes:

Recommend this book to:

Title: The Long Tail: Why the Future of Business is Selling Less of More	

Author: Chris Anderson

Paperback   Hardback   Audio   E-Book

Dates:	Source:
Started -	☐ Bought:
Finished -	☐ Loaned From:

Why I read this book:

This book has inspired me to read/learn/visit:

Notes:

Great Quotes:

Recommend this book to:

Title: Too Big to Fail: The Inside Story of How Wall Street and Washington Fought to Save the Financial System from Crisis — and Themselves
Author: Andrew Ross Sorkin

Paperback   Hardback   Audio   E-Book

Dates: Started - Finished -	Source: ❏ Bought: ❏ Loaned From:

Why I read this book:
This book has inspired me to read/learn/visit:
Notes:
Great Quotes:
Recommend this book to:

Title: What to Say When You Talk to Your Self

Author: Shad Helmstetter

Paperback   Hardback   Audio   E-Book

Dates: Started - Finished -	Source: ☐ Bought: ☐ Loaned From:

Why I read this book:

This book has inspired me to read/learn/visit:

Notes:

Great Quotes:

Recommend this book to:

Title: The Extremely Successful Salesman's Club	
Author: Chris Murray	

Paperback   Hardback   Audio   E-Book

Dates: Started - Finished -	Source: ☐ Bought: ☐ Loaned From:

Why I read this book:

This book has inspired me to read/learn/visit:

Notes:

Great Quotes:

Recommend this book to:

Title: The Secrets of Consulting: A Guide to Giving and Getting Advice Successfully

Author: Gerald M. Weinberg

Paperback   Hardback   Audio   E-Book

Dates: Started - Finished -	Source: ❑ Bought: ❑ Loaned From:

Why I read this book:

This book has inspired me to read/learn/visit:

Notes:

Great Quotes:

Recommend this book to:

Title: Peopleware: Productive Projects and Teams

Author: Tom DeMarco

Paperback	Hardback	Audio	E-Book

Dates:
  Started -
  Finished -
	Source:
	  ❑ Bought:
	  ❑ Loaned From:

Why I read this book:

This book has inspired me to read/learn/visit:

Notes:

Great Quotes:

Recommend this book to:

Title: The Effective Executive: The Definitive Guide to Getting the Right Things Done

Author: Peter F. Drucker

Paperback   Hardback   Audio   E-Book

Dates:
  Started -
  Finished -

Source:
  ❑ Bought:
  ❑ Loaned From:

Why I read this book:

This book has inspired me to read/learn/visit:

Notes:

Great Quotes:

Recommend this book to:

Title: Shoe Dog: A Memoir by the Creator of NIKE

Author: Phil Knight

Paperback   Hardback   Audio   E-Book

Dates:	Source:
Started -	☐ Bought:
Finished -	☐ Loaned From:

Why I read this book:

This book has inspired me to read/learn/visit:

Notes:

Great Quotes:

Recommend this book to:

Title: Great by Choice: Uncertainty, Chaos, and Luck—Why Some Thrive Despite Them All

Author: James C. Collins

Paperback   Hardback   Audio   E-Book

Dates:
 Started -
 Finished -

Source:
 ❏ Bought:
 ❏ Loaned From:

Why I read this book:

This book has inspired me to read/learn/visit:

Notes:

Great Quotes:

Recommend this book to:

Title: The Undercover Economist	

Author: Tim Harford

Paperback	Hardback	Audio	E-Book

Dates:
  Started -
  Finished -
	Source:
	☐ Bought:
	☐ Loaned From:

Why I read this book:

This book has inspired me to read/learn/visit:

Notes:

Great Quotes:

Recommend this book to:

Title: Confessions of a Public Speaker

Author: Scott Berkun

Paperback   Hardback   Audio   E-Book

Dates:
 Started -
 Finished -

Source:
 ❑ Bought:
 ❑ Loaned From:

Why I read this book:

This book has inspired me to read/learn/visit:

Notes:

Great Quotes:

Recommend this book to:

Title: Never Work Again: Work Less, Earn More and Live Your Freedom	
Author: Erlend Bakke	

Paperback   Hardback   Audio   E-Book

Dates:
  Started -
  Finished -
	Source:
	❑ Bought:
	❑ Loaned From:

Why I read this book:

This book has inspired me to read/learn/visit:

Notes:

Great Quotes:

Recommend this book to:

Title: Eat That Frog!: 21 Great Ways to Stop Procrastinating and Get More Done in Less Time

Author: Brian Tracy

Paperback   Hardback   Audio   E-Book

Dates:
 Started -
 Finished -

Source:
 ❑ Bought:
 ❑ Loaned From:

Why I read this book:

This book has inspired me to read/learn/visit:

Notes:

Great Quotes:

Recommend this book to:

Title: Principles of Marketing	

Author: Philip Kotler	

Paperback   Hardback   Audio   E-Book

Dates: Started - Finished -	Source: ❑ Bought: ❑ Loaned From:

Why I read this book:

This book has inspired me to read/learn/visit:

Notes:

Great Quotes:

Recommend this book to:

Title: The Contrarian's Guide to Leadership	
Author: Steven B. Sample	

Paperback   Hardback   Audio   E-Book

Dates:
  Started -
  Finished -
	Source:
	❏ Bought:
	❏ Loaned From:

Why I read this book:

This book has inspired me to read/learn/visit:

Notes:

Great Quotes:

Recommend this book to:

Title: The Ten-Day MBA : A Step-By-Step Guide To Mastering The Skills Taught In America's Top Business Schools	

Author: Steven Silbiger

Paperback   Hardback   Audio   E-Book

Dates:
  Started -
  Finished -
	Source:
	❑ Bought:
	❑ Loaned From:

Why I read this book:

This book has inspired me to read/learn/visit:

Notes:

Great Quotes:

Recommend this book to:

Title: Orbiting the Giant Hairball: A Corporate Fool's Guide to Surviving with Grace

Author: Gordon MacKenzie

Paperback   Hardback   Audio   E-Book

Dates:
  Started -
  Finished -

Source:
  ❑   Bought:
  ❑   Loaned From:

Why I read this book:

This book has inspired me to read/learn/visit:

Notes:

Great Quotes:

Recommend this book to:

Title: Social Media for the Executive	

Author: Brian E. Boyd Sr.

Paperback	Hardback	Audio	E-Book

Dates:
  Started -
  Finished -
	Source:
	  ❏ Bought:
	  ❏ Loaned From:

Why I read this book:

This book has inspired me to read/learn/visit:

Notes:

Great Quotes:

Recommend this book to:

Title: The Power of Full Engagement: Managing Energy, Not Time, Is the Key to High Performance and Personal Renewal

Author: Jim Loehr

Paperback   Hardback   Audio   E-Book

Dates:
 Started -
 Finished -

Source:
❏ Bought:
❏ Loaned From:

Why I read this book:

This book has inspired me to read/learn/visit:

Notes:

Great Quotes:

Recommend this book to:

Title: EntreLeadership: 20 Years of Practical Business Wisdom from the Trenches	
Author: Dave Ramsey	

Paperback   Hardback   Audio   E-Book

Dates:
  Started -
  Finished -
	Source:
	  ❑ Bought:
	  ❑ Loaned From:

Why I read this book:

This book has inspired me to read/learn/visit:

Notes:

Great Quotes:

Recommend this book to:

Title: Launching a Leadership Revolution: Mastering the Five Levels of Influence

Author: Chris Brady

Paperback   Hardback   Audio   E-Book

Dates:
  Started -
  Finished -

Source:
❏ Bought:
❏ Loaned From:

Why I read this book:

This book has inspired me to read/learn/visit:

Notes:

Great Quotes:

Recommend this book to:

Title: Difficult Conversations: How to Discuss What Matters Most

Author: Douglas Stone

Paperback   Hardback   Audio   E-Book

Dates:
  Started -
  Finished -

Source:
  ❏ Bought:
  ❏ Loaned From:

Why I read this book:

This book has inspired me to read/learn/visit:

Notes:

Great Quotes:

Recommend this book to:

Title: Capitalism and Freedom

Author: Milton Friedman

Paperback　　Hardback　　Audio　　E-Book

Dates: 　Started - 　Finished -	Source: ❏　　Bought: ❏　　Loaned From:

Why I read this book:

This book has inspired me to read/learn/visit:

Notes:

Great Quotes:

Recommend this book to:

Title: From the Ground Up: A Journey to Reimagine the Promise of America

Author: Howard Schultz

Paperback   Hardback   Audio   E-Book

Dates:
  Started -
  Finished -
	Source:
	❑ Bought:
	❑ Loaned From:

Why I read this book:

This book has inspired me to read/learn/visit:

Notes:

Great Quotes:

Recommend this book to:

Title: It Is What It Is, Or Is It....: All About Business

Author: Cathy Snelgrove Jeff Roziere

Paperback   Hardback   Audio   E-Book

Dates:
 Started -
 Finished -

Source:
❑ Bought:
❑ Loaned From:

Why I read this book:

This book has inspired me to read/learn/visit:

Notes:

Great Quotes:

Recommend this book to:

Title: The Idea-Driven Organization: Unlocking the Power in Bottom-Up Ideas	

Author: Alan G. Robinson

Paperback   Hardback   Audio   E-Book

Dates:
  Started -
  Finished -
	Source:
	❑ Bought:
	❑ Loaned From:

Why I read this book:

This book has inspired me to read/learn/visit:

Notes:

Great Quotes:

Recommend this book to:

Title: Match in the Root Cellar: How You Can Spark a Peak Performance Culture	

Author: Chris McGoff

Paperback   Hardback   Audio   E-Book

Dates:
  Started -
  Finished -
	Source:
	❑ Bought:
	❑ Loaned From:

Why I read this book:

This book has inspired me to read/learn/visit:

Notes:

Great Quotes:

Recommend this book to:

Alphabetical By Title

Against the Gods: The Remarkable Story of Risk
All Marketers Are Liars
Blue Ocean Strategy: How to Create Uncontested Market Space and Make the Competition Irrelevant
Built to Last: Successful Habits of Visionary Companies
Business Model Generation
Capitalism and Freedom
Competitive Advantage: Creating and Sustaining Superior Performance
Confessions of a Public Speaker
Crossing the Chasm: Marketing and Selling High-Tech Products to Mainstream Customers
Crucial Conversations: Tools for Talking When Stakes Are High
Dare to Lead
Delivering Happiness: A Path to Profits, Passion, and Purpose
Difficult Conversations: How to Discuss What Matters Most
Drive: The Surprising Truth About What Motivates Us
Eat That Frog!: 21 Great Ways to Stop Procrastinating and Get More Done in Less Time
Emotional Intelligence 2.0
EntreLeadership: 20 Years of Practical Business Wisdom from the Trenches
Explosive Growth: A Few Things I Learned While Growing To 100 Million Users - And Losing $78 Million
First, Break All the Rules: What the World's Greatest Managers Do Differently
Founders at Work: Stories of Startups' Early Days
Freakonomics: A Rogue Economist Explores the Hidden Side of Everything
Free: The Future of a Radical Price

From the Ground Up: A Journey to Reimagine the Promise of America
Getting Things Done: The Art of Stress-Free Productivity
Getting to Yes: Negotiating Agreement Without Giving In
Good to Great: Why Some Companies Make the Leap... and Others Don't
Great by Choice: Uncertainty, Chaos, and Luck—Why Some Thrive Despite Them All
How to Win Friends and Influence People
In Search of Excellence
Influence: The Psychology of Persuasion
It Is What It Is, Or Is It....: All About Business
Launching a Leadership Revolution: Mastering the Five Levels of Influence
Liar's Poker
Linchpin: Are You Indispensable?
Made to Stick: Why Some Ideas Survive and Others Die
Marketing Management
Massive Action Equal Massive Results: Learn the Critical Mental Framework to Focus Your Energy, Reach Your Goals Quicker and Live an Insanely Awesome Life
Match in the Root Cellar: How You Can Spark a Peak Performance Culture
Moneyball: The Art of Winning an Unfair Game
Never Eat Alone: And Other Secrets to Success, One Relationship at a Time
Never Work Again: Work Less, Earn More and Live Your Freedom
Orbiting the Giant Hairball: A Corporate Fool's Guide to Surviving with Grace

Organisational Anatomy
Outliers: The Story of Success
Peopleware: Productive Projects and Teams
Positioning: The Battle for Your Mind: How to Be Seen and Heard in the Overcrowded Marketplace
Predictably Irrational: The Hidden Forces That Shape Our Decisions
Principles of Marketing
Purple Cow: Transform Your Business by Being Remarkable
Quiet: The Power of Introverts in a World That Can't Stop Talking
Rework
Rich Dad, Poor Dad
Secret to Startup Failure: Fail Fast. Fail Cheap. Fail Happy.
Shoe Dog: A Memoir by the Creator of NIKE
Social Media for the Executive
Start with Why: How Great Leaders Inspire Everyone to Take Action
Steve Jobs
Strengths Finder 2.0
SuperFreakonomics: Global Cooling, Patriotic Prostitutes And Why Suicide Bombers Should Buy Life Insurance
The 21 Irrefutable Laws of Leadership: Follow Them and People Will Follow You
The 4-Hour Workweek
The 48 Laws of Power
The 7 Habits of Highly Effective People: Powerful Lessons in Personal Change
The Art of the Start: The Time-Tested, Battle-Hardened Guide for Anyone Starting Anything
The Art of War

The Art of War
The Autobiography of Benjamin Franklin
The Big Short: Inside the Doomsday Machine
The Black Swan: The Impact of the Highly Improbable
The Contrarian's Guide to Leadership
The Dip: A Little Book That Teaches You When to Quit
The E-Myth Revisited: Why Most Small Businesses Don't Work and What to Do About It
The Effective Executive: The Definitive Guide to Getting the Right Things Done
The Extremely Successful Salesman's Club
The Five Dysfunctions of a Team: A Leadership Fable
The Goal: A Process of Ongoing Improvement
The Greatest Salesman in the World
The Idea-Driven Organization: Unlocking the Power in Bottom-Up Ideas
The Innovator's Dilemma: The Revolutionary Book that Will Change the Way You Do Business
The Intelligent Investor
The Lean Startup: How Today's Entrepreneurs Use Continuous Innovation to Create Radically Successful Businesses
The Long Tail: Why the Future of Business is Selling Less of More
The Millionaire Mind
The One Minute Manager
The Power of Full Engagement: Managing Energy, Not Time, Is the Key to High Performance and Personal Renewal
The Richest Man in Babylon

The Secrets of Consulting: A Guide to Giving and Getting Advice Successfully
The Speed of Trust: The One Thing that Changes Everything
The Ten-Day MBA : A Step-By-Step Guide To Mastering The Skills Taught In America's Top Business Schools
The Tipping Point: How Little Things Can Make a Big Difference
The Undercover Economist
The World Is Flat: A Brief History of the Twenty-first Century
Think and Grow Rich
Thinking, Fast and Slow
Too Big to Fail: The Inside Story of How Wall Street and Washington Fought to Save the Financial System from Crisis — and Themselves
Tribes We Need You to Lead Us. Seth Godin
What to Say When You Talk to Your Self
When Genius Failed: The Rise and Fall of Long-Term Capital Management
Winning Intl
You Couldn't Have Told Me Before I Started My Business?
Zig Ziglar's Secrets of Closing the Sale

NOTES

NOTES

NOTES

NOTES

NOTES

NOTES

NOTES

NOTES

NOTES

www.ingramcontent.com/pod-product-compliance
Lightning Source LLC
Chambersburg PA
CBHW021830170526
45157CB00007B/2740